A special gift for

_____

With love

_____

Date

_____

Look for these other *Hugs* books:

Hugs for Nurses
Hugs for Heroes
Hugs for Women
Hugs for Sisters
Hugs for Grandma
Hugs for Friends
Hugs for Girlfriends
Hugs for New Moms
Hugs for Mom
Hugs for Daughters
Hugs for Grads
Hugs for Kids
Hugs for Teens
Hugs for Teachers
Hugs for Those in Love
Hugs for the Hurting
Hugs for Grandparents
Hugs for Dad
Hugs for Women on the Go
Hugs for the Holidays
Hugs to Encourage and Inspire

Stories, sayings, and scriptures to Encourage and Inspire

hugs™

for

friends

book 2

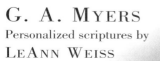

G. A. MYERS

Personalized scriptures by
LEANN WEISS

Our purpose at Howard Publishing is to:

- *Increase faith* in the hearts of growing Christians
- *Inspire holiness* in the lives of believers
- *Instill hope* in the hearts of struggling people everywhere

Because He's coming again!

Hugs for Friends, Book 2 © 2003 by G. A. Myers
All rights reserved. Printed in the United States of America
Published by Howard Publishing Co., Inc.
3117 North 7th Street, West Monroe, LA 71291-2227

04 05 06 07 08 09 10 11 12   10 9 8 7 6 5

Paraphrased scriptures © 2003 LeAnn Weiss, 3006 Brandywine Dr.,
Orlando, FL 32806; 407-898-4410

Edited by Between the Lines
Interior design by Stephanie Denney

Library of Congress Cataloging-in-Publication Data

Myers, G. A., 1955–
   Hugs for friends book 2 : stories, sayings, and scriptures to encourage and
inspire / G. A. Myers ; personalized scriptures by LeAnn Weiss.—[New ed.].
   p. cm.
   ISBN 1-58229-298-1
   1. Friendship—Religious aspects—Christianity. I. Title: Hugs for friends
book two. II. Weiss, LeAnn. III. Title.

BV45647.F7 M935 2003
241'.6762—dc21

                                                              2002038764

CONTENTS

Chapter One: Timing 1

Chapter Two: Companionship 19

Chapter Three: Commitment. 37

Chapter Four: Involvement 55

Chapter Five: Sacrifice 71

Chapter Six: Dependability. 89

Chapter Seven: Faithfulness 105

*In the sweetness
of friendship let there be
laughter, and sharing
of pleasures. For in the dew
of little things the heart finds
its morning and is refreshed.*

Kahlil Gibran

Chapter One

Timing

the selecting of the best time
or speed for doing something in order to
achieve the desired or maximum result

*L*ift your eyes up
and *remember* that your
help comes from *Me*.

I take **hold**
of your right *hand*
and remind you **not to fear**
because *I will help* you.

*W*atch **Me** make all things
beautiful
in My **perfect** timing.

Almighty God

LOVING YOU,

Your
Almighty
God

—from Psalm 121:1–2; Isaiah 41:13; Ecclesiastes 3:11

The Scriptures say that God saved us *"at just the right time"* (Romans 5:6). He knows the importance of timing. That's why He sends us the friends we need at just the right time—to fill the gaps, hear our gripes, and strengthen us when we want to give up.

Is there anything more pleasant than the voice of a friend when we're feeling the full weight of failure and frustration? That sound alone can bring hope to a surrendered heart.

Is there anything more comforting than the arm of a friend steadying us when we become weak-kneed from the stress and strain of life's weight on our shoulders? That helpful arm serves to remind us that we don't have to face tomorrow alone.

Friends seem to appear out of nowhere when we need them most—to reinforce us for unexpected or extended battle. They come without fear for themselves, because they know sacrifice is part of the friendship. They come to walk with us, side by side and step by step, until we find a way to defeat the enemy.

Every time a friend rescues us at just the right time, another memory is made. Celebrate those memories often. Lift those diamond-bright moments to the light and be thankful for the pressures that brought them into existence. Above all, don't forget to thank God. He was the one who knew exactly the right time to send you a friend.

God pairs people as friends

at the right time and

pace and season of need.

Wayne Watson

*T*hough Kim was taken aback
by Sherry's brashness and honesty,
she found herself drawn to her.

A Friend in the Clutch

It started on a chilly, windy day in Wichita, Kansas. The two young women didn't plan to get to know each other well, much less become good friends. Kim Logan was rushing from her apartment to her car to get to class at Wichita State University. She had the biggest exam of the semester in fifteen minutes, and she wanted to get there in time to look over her notes again. Distracted with juggling her books while reviewing in her mind what she had stayed up half the night to study, she didn't notice Sherry Brown until she bumped into her. Sherry was rubbing sleep from her heavy-lidded brown eyes and stretching in preparation for the mile walk to her first class of the day.

The girls were acquainted. Sherry lived downstairs in the red brick apartment complex, and Kim lived on the upper level right above her. Until today, their only real interaction had been several small confrontations over Sherry's music, which was always too loud for Kim. That was the number one reason Kim didn't plan to get to know Sherry better. Sherry liked her music the way she liked her life: loud, fun, and full of flare. Her major was marketing, and she liked the fast pace that accompanied her creative opportunities.

Kim, on the other hand, was a self-proclaimed nerd majoring in English literature. She loved solitude, meditation, prayer, and reading. Her idea of a great weekend was walking through quiet woods and talking to God or curling up with a hefty classic tome, which, she suspected, Sherry would find useful only as a doorstop.

On her way to the car that day, Kim made a halfhearted stab at being friendly and said hello to Sherry. Never shy,

Sherry took the opportunity to ask for a ride to the campus. Caught off guard, Kim hesitated for just a moment, then agreed. "OK," she said, then added quickly, "but I control the volume on the radio."

"As long as we don't have to listen to Bach or BEEthoven," Sherry laughed, exaggerating for fun.

"I'm surprised you even know they existed," Kim shot back.

"Oooooh," Sherry responded. "That was witty, Miss Kim. There may be hope for you—you could have a sense of humor behind those wire-rimmed glasses!"

"For someone begging a ride, you're pretty lippy," Kim remarked.

"You're right, there," Sherry admitted honestly. "In fact, 'Lippy' is my middle name. My mom tells me that if she had a nickel for every time I mouthed off, she'd be a millionaire. I'm sorry. If I promise to tone it down a bit, could I still have that ride?"

Though Kim was taken aback first by Sherry's brashness and then by her honesty, she found herself drawn to Sherry.

"Sure, but I still get to control the radio." The two shared a chuckle.

Kim slid into the driver's seat of the Toyota Celica and turned the key. The engine didn't roar to life as she expected it to. It was so silent she could hear the click of the key turning in the ignition. "What in the world…" Kim trailed off, puzzled.

Sherry covered her face with her hands. "Uh-oh," she said softly. "Check your lights. You probably left them on all night."

Amazed at Sherry's instinctive response, Kim glanced at the knob and realized Sherry was right. "Oh no," Kim moaned. "What'll I do? I can't miss that test!"

Tears formed in Kim's eyes as she hastily grabbed her books. She'd have to run the mile to campus.

"Hey, hold on there, Kimmy," Sherry said as if she were pulling back the reins of a horse. "Don't you know you can start a stick shift by popping the clutch?"

Kim looked at her with a puzzled expression. "No, I've never even heard of popping a clutch."

"What was I thinking! Guys like Twain and Dickens don't write about things like that," Sherry said with good-natured sarcasm. "Here's how it's done: I'll get out and push the car until it picks up a little speed while you sit there and hold the clutch in. When I yell 'pop the clutch,' you let it out fast, and it'll start right up. Got it?"

"I think so," Kim replied with genuine awe.

Sherry got behind the car and went through a checklist with Kim. "First gear, check?"

Kim shouted back, "Check!"

"Brake off, check?" Sherry continued.

"Check!" Kim echoed loudly.

"Clutch in, check?" Sherry finished.

"Check!" Kim shouted.

"All systems are go!" Sherry yelled cheerfully.

Sherry pushed with all of her might, and the car began to creep forward, slowly at first, then picking up speed. Kim sat frozen in her seat until Sherry screamed at the top of her lungs, "Pop the stupid clutch!"

As soon as Kim complied, the car lurched forward and

startled her so badly she slammed on the brakes. Sherry went flying up onto the trunk of the car. A frightened Kim looked in her rearview mirror to see Sherry, red-faced, sprawled across the trunk and on the rear window.

"Are you all right?" Kim yelled. "I'm so sorry, Sherry. I'm so sorry!"

To her shock and relief, Kim discovered that Sherry was laughing hysterically. "That was absolutely the shabbiest attempt at clutch-popping I've ever witnessed," Sherry gasped between outbursts of laughter.

Emerging from the car, Kim joined in the laughter. "It was pretty comical to see you take flight and land on my trunk that way," she told Sherry, making an arc through the air with one hand.

"Yeah, I'm sure I looked like a bird."

"More like an airborne ostrich. Your legs were everywhere!"

They laughed for several minutes before Sherry spoke with mock indignation. "Hey, why am I laughing?" she harrumphed. "I just realized you let the car die. Now we have to do the whole thing over again."

They looked at each other for a split second, then screamed with laughter again.

Kim looked sheepishly at Sherry. "Do you want me to push this time and let you pop the clutch?"

"No, Kimmy, my friend," Sherry said patiently. "I want you to learn to get it right. Hop back in there, and let's try it again."

They went through the checklist one more time with an added reminder to keep the car running after Kim popped the clutch. Then Sherry started pushing. "Pop the clutch, girl, pop the clutch," she yelled.

This time Kim performed her task perfectly, and the engine roared to life.

Sherry hopped into the car and rubbed her palms together gleefully. "You'll never learn that in one of your books," she told Kim, who nodded in agreement.

"You know," Sherry continued thoughtfully, "I can tell you need taking care of. I think I'll nominate myself for the job. You live in a world of books and imagination where smart people express ideas in words. I live in the real world where people have to be street-smart. I could use some help with my study skills, and trust me, you could use some tips on your social skills," she giggled, teasingly. "Let's get you to class. After all, you can't miss the most important test of the year."

After class they met for lunch—an appointment that soon turned into a daily event. Their respect for each other grew as each helped the other discover a world she never knew existed. They dreamed together, hoped together, and always took care of each other. Together they built a friendship that would last a lifetime.

Whenever differences threatened their closeness, they would recall the morning when two opposite personalities became lifelong friends over a stalled car and a popped clutch, and they would laugh until they cried.

Chapter Two

Companionship

the state of being with someone;
the relationship as companions

*W*hen you come **near** to Me,
I'm so *close* to you.

*T*here's **no** darkness in Me.
I fill you with *joy*
in My **presence** and *bless you*
with *eternal* pleasures
at My right **hand.**

*M*ay you walk in
My *light,*
experiencing *sweet* fellowship
with **friends**
as My Son's **blood**
purifies you.

Father of Light

SHINING ON YOU,

Your
Father
of Light

—from James 4:8; Psalm 16:11; 1 John 1:5–7

No modern medicine or meditation has quite the same healing effect as a friend. Friends can take the space once occupied by loneliness and fill it to the brim with partnership and purpose. Isolation is replaced by delightful companionship. Heartache is healed by the joy and satisfaction of camaraderie.

Only a soul mate can fill the need in each of us for true companionship—the craving to be known, understood, and valued. And that kind of friendship is a rare gift. But when that treasure is found, it works its way into our lives, into the deepest recesses of our hearts. Companionship can transform us. It replaces selfishness with a spirit of sacrifice. It soothes the sadness of loss and raises a song of joy. It buries the hatchet of hatred and reaps a harvest of love.

The wonderful, miraculous thing about friendship is, anyone can participate. Each of us has the power to partner with another and, in so doing, change the world one heart at a time. You, as a friend, have that power. Your companionship can bring peace and joy to another.

Companionship does require an investment. It takes time to build. You'll have to share your pain and loss, even reveal your weaknesses. But the rewards are worth it, because companionship means not only bearing one another's burdens but also sharing in victories, in healing, in joy. And in a world fueled by greed, selfishness, and hatred, friendship—companionship—may be the only way to make a difference.

A friend is someone

who shares with you a smile,

a tear, a hand.

Conover

The thought of living without
her friend brought waves
of anxiety and desperation.

Toe to Toe

*H*elen stood and gazed longingly out the glassed wall that stretched all the way up to the cathedral ceiling in her great room. It was Thanksgiving and darkness had already begun to cling to the freshly fallen snow. She could see the different hues of light thrown off by neighboring houses that were already covered with the small multicolor lights that blinked and danced in the night and signaled the coming of Christmas. Although this was normally one of her favorite times of year, she could find no reason for joy now. She felt alone, unwanted, and dispirited. Her best friend had died six weeks earlier, and she was having a hard time adjusting to the silence and the sadness. She tugged absently at her shoulder-length gray hair and thought about Connie.

Connie was more than a friend; she was a soul mate and confidante who had faced the best and worst of times with Helen. They had met at St. Andrews Hospital fifteen years earlier when Helen's husband, Harley, was being treated for cancer. Connie was a volunteer who loved bringing some measure of comfort to the patients and their families. She had taken up the job after her own husband died of cancer, and she was deeply loved and appreciated in the hospital by staff and patients alike.

Helen, however, didn't much like Connie when they first met. The tall Texan was loud and loving, but Helen was a quiet southern belle not given to boisterous displays of affection. She shunned Connie's attempts at friendship by ignoring her. That, however, only fueled Connie's determination. Connie brought small gifts and hugged her even though Helen wouldn't respond. Connie would tap her toe three times on the top of Helen's toe and say, "When you get tired of carrying your heartache alone, we can walk through it together." Helen would simply lower her eyes until Connie walked away.

Yet when Harley's struggle with cancer ended, Helen felt so alone and overwhelmed that she turned to Connie for comfort. "I can't bear this alone. Would you help me get through it?" she pleaded softly. Without saying a word, Connie tapped the familiar three times on her toe, then gathered Helen in a gentle hug. This time, Helen crumpled into Connie's arms and wept for an hour.

After that the two became close friends and partners in encouragement. Anytime a need arose in the small town, the two of them pitched in to help. Helen and Connie came to respect and treasure their different personalities. They enjoyed volunteering together so much that after about a year, they decided to sell their respective homes and purchase one together so they could be closer to the hospital and could open their home to parents of children who were undergoing treatment. Time with Connie was full of friendship, fun, and fruitful labor. The two women were like children, laughing loudly, playing good-natured pranks, and doing good deeds.

At Christmastime last year, Connie began showing the first signs of her illness. It didn't stop them from delivering the gifts they had gathered for needy children in the area, but by New Year's Day, Connie was feeling weak. The next Monday she consulted her doctor, who sent her to the hospital for testing. The diagnosis was devastating. Connie had advanced colon cancer.

Connie faced her future with courage, but Helen struggled. At times the thought of living life without her friend brought waves of anxiety and desperation. Connie almost always sensed her panic and would tap her slippered foot softly on Helen's toe. "We'll walk through this together, my friend," she promised.

It was early October when Connie neared the end of her battle. Helen made her as comfortable as possible, but Connie's concern was that Helen not be lonely or lose what had become her purpose in life. One afternoon she asked Helen to bring her the phone and leave her alone. About two hours later, she called her friend back into the room.

"What were you doing in here all that time?" Helen quizzed her.

Connie slid her leg from the bed, tapped her toe on Helen's, and said, "Don't worry, my friend. We'll walk through this together."

One week later, Connie died peacefully in her sleep. Helen tried to keep up the good work she and Connie had done together, but each day her grief and loneliness made it harder and harder until she finally retreated into the quiet shelter of her home.

Now, on Thanksgiving, she felt the full weight of her grief. The loneliness left her feeling more desolate than ever. Suddenly a sharp knock on the front door echoed through the empty house. At first she tried to ignore it. The knock came again, louder. Helen looked out her front window to see a young man in a snowy beard, overalls, and heavy boots standing at her door with two large packages.

Chapter Two: *companionship*

She opened the door slightly and saw on the street a white van with the words "Heavenly Ham" painted on the side. "Mrs. Chamberlain?" The man asked hesitantly. "Helen Chamberlain?"

"Yes, I'm Helen Chamberlain," she answered with reservation.

"I'm sure glad your home, ma'am. I've got three turkeys and fixings enough for an army out here in the van." He stepped into the house with two wrapped turkeys before she could object.

"There must be some mistake—I didn't order any turkeys, and I certainly don't need three of them," Helen protested.

"No, I know you didn't order them. Connie Howser ordered them almost two months ago and said they were to be delivered at 5 P.M. sharp on Thanksgiving Day."

Helen looked as though she had just seen an angel. "Connie called you and did what?"

"Yes ma'am, she gave strict instructions about everything. She said they were to be here right at five o'clock because a bunch of people would be here for Thanksgiving dinner." Placing the turkeys on the table, the man looked around with a puzzled expression. "Did people forget to come, ma'am?"

"No, I didn't invite anyone," Helen answered sharply.

Embarrassed, the deliveryman excused himself to get the rest of the meal from the truck.

"Just what are you up to, Connie Howser?" Helen whispered to herself.

The young man returned with arms laden. "I think your guests have arrived," he announced.

Helen rushed to the door and opened it to see Amy, a nurse from the cancer ward, leading a crowd of people up the sidewalk to the house. When she reached the door she smiled broadly and said, "Hey, Helen, Connie invited all the families in the cancer ward, along with any patients who felt up to it, to come over for Thanksgiving dinner. She said you'd have it all set up and I would disappoint you terribly if I didn't bring everyone I could."

Amy noticed tears spilling down Helen's face and whispered, "You OK, Helen?"

Chapter Two: *companionship*

"Oh yes, I'm fine. Come on in here and get warm. The food is being set up now, and we can give thanks and eat in just a few minutes."

Helen stepped away into another room and spoke as though Connie were there with her. "Thank you for the gift, my friend. I feel the tap of your toe."

She looked back at the crowd that had gathered in the living room where she and Connie had comforted so many grieving friends and families. Dozens of guests stood or sat, some with blank stares, others wringing their hands, still others with worry etched in their faces. Helen wiped away her tears and entered the room with a hearty smile.

"Welcome, my friends. I'm glad to have you here on this Thanksgiving Day, and I want all of you to feel free to visit again whenever you need a friend to help carry your load. My name is Helen, and I'll be that friend."

After a prayer of thanks the group began moving into the dining room. One woman stayed behind, staring out the window. She was middle-aged and thin, with shoulders that sagged under the weight of her sorrow. Helen quietly joined her and asked her name.

"Darla Hayes," the woman answered softly, reluctantly. "My husband is in the hospital and probably won't make it through Christmas. I don't even know what I'm doing here."

Helen remembered the pain she had felt when she lost her husband, and she remembered how Connie had helped her make it through. She took Darla gently by the shoulders and turned her so she could look into her eyes. "You may not know why you're here, but I do." She tapped her toe on Darla's and said, "Don't worry. We'll walk through this together."

Chapter Three

Commitment

a pledge or promise;
obligation

*E*xperience My everlasting arms.
My *Spirit* made you,
and My **breath** gives you *life*.

I am your **trustworthy** refuge.
When you make *Me*
and My ways your **priority**,
I'll take care of all your needs
through My unlimited **riches** in *glory*.

*A*nd don't forget…
you can do *all things*
because *Christ* is your unfailing
power
source.

Heavenly Father

HOLDING YOU,

Your
Heavenly
Father

—from Deuteronomy 33:27; Job 33:4; Philippians 4:13, 19

What is it that makes you the best of friends? What is it about you that brings out the best in others?

It could be your willingness to engage the lives of your friends wherever they are. You willingly enter their war zones and fight the daily battles with words of encouragement and comfort. No fight is too small or too big for you when it comes to your friends.

It could be the help you offer others climbing the mountain of faith. You anchor those pushing themselves to the summit. You refuse to leave anyone behind. You won't give up until everyone reaches the goal.

Perhaps most important is the deep connection you eagerly seek to have with others. It's an invisible link of friendship that unites your heart with the hearts of others. It's powerful enough to hold lives together no matter what may come along. Nothing can shake you loose from those you call friends. No one can come between you and those you love. Nothing can separate you.

In a world of shallow commitments and abandoned loyalties, your devotion is unique and rare. You are locked in for the long haul. You're staying no matter who else goes. You've wrapped yourself around the hearts of your friends with an embrace that will hold through any storm.

What is it that makes you the best of friends? The answer is simple: commitment. Your commitment to others makes you a friend par excellence!

*R*eal friendship

is shown in times

of trouble.

Euripides

$\mathcal{S}$am rammed his car into the speeding
auto, pushing it into the median before
it could reach the children.

Blood Brothers

*T*hree weathered men shuffled into the downtown doughnut shop with tired faces and swollen eyes. They had many good reasons for congregating every Tuesday morning for their favorite brew and pastry, but the thing that summoned these long-term friends today was not good and not welcome. Someone was missing. Someone with whom they had served in World War II on a bomber they had christened the *Wind Walker*.

Chapter Three: *commitment*

The first man, Alton, had been a gunner, and a mighty good one, to hear the old men talk. He could wedge his thin frame into the tightest crevice and still find room to maneuver. He hadn't changed much through the years. He had gained just ten pounds since his air force days, and his youthful spirit still shone from his ocean-blue eyes.

Sonny, the other gunner, had not fared as well. Although he had retained his athletic physique, he bore the marks of a hard life—lines of care were etched deeply in his face.

Blake was the youngest, and he looked it. The navigator for the flying fortress possessed unusual energy and an infectious laugh.

Each ordered their "usual" and found a seat. "I want to order one for Sam," Sonny announced. "It's just not the same without him. Maybe it'll make him feel closer." Sonny went to the counter and requested one more coffee and doughnut, just the way Sam would have ordered it.

Sam's absence was the reason for their shared sorrow. He had been the pilot of the great bomber they'd flown for two years. He had remained the leader of this band of veterans ever since. It was he who initiated the routine of visiting the neighborhood coffee shop to relive the old stories. But today he couldn't join them. Sam was in the hospital, fighting for his life.

It had been more an act of heroism than an accident. Sam had been driving on the busy interstate. A drunk driver was weaving dangerously. Sam looked ahead and saw a school bus stalled by the side of the road and surrounded by children. The erratic car was careening directly toward the kids.

With the keen skills and instincts of a pilot, Sam rammed his car into the side of the speeding auto, pushing it into the median before it could reach the children. With a thundering crash, Sam's car flipped over, then came to rest right-side up.

The teacher who witnessed the incident told emergency workers that Sam had saved their lives. No one could yet tell whether the unconscious hero had done so at the cost of his own life. When Sam's wife, Lil, called Alton with the news, he'd called the friends together. They had kept vigil at the hospital while they waited for news from Sam's surgeon.

They knew Sam would have despised their "creative conversation" while time passed in the waiting room. Sam had saved each of their lives in separate incidents during the war. Every time they shared their favorite stories, Sam noticed that his comrades got more "creative" in how they remembered the details. He once told them that if he were half the man they made him out to be, he wouldn't have needed a plane—he could have just flapped his arms, dropped bombs from his armpits, and won the war single-handedly.

But Alton, Sonny, and Blake knew that Sam really had saved their necks on many occasions, and no amount of humility on his part would make them forget it or stop recounting it. The three of them had been afraid that they'd never get a chance to return Sam's favors. Now they all felt powerless to help the friend who lay near death.

It was nearly midnight when the surgeon came to talk with the anxious group about Sam's prognosis. The news was bleak. Sam was bleeding internally, and they were having difficulty pinpointing the problem. Sam needed a transfusion fast.

At this news, everyone in the room took a deep breath. Lil and the friends knew what it meant. Sam had an extremely rare blood type. The small-town hospital had none on hand.

They had already begun searching for possible donors in the area. Within thirty minutes the answer came, but with little comfort. One donor, Lloyd Simpson, lived an hour north in the tiny community of Portland, but every attempt to reach him had been fruitless.

Blake spoke up first. "Let's get in a car and go after this guy," he urged the others. "We owe it to Sam to find him and get him here."

"It'll be two o'clock in the morning by the time we get there," Sonny protested. "What are we going to do, roust this guy out of bed and drag him to the hospital?"

Alton and Blake looked at each other. In unison, they said, "That's exactly what we'll do."

Chapter Three: *commitment*

The three friends piled into Alton's Buick Roadmaster. They peeled out of the parking lot and headed for Portland on their most important mission in nearly sixty years. They would do whatever it took to bring Sam home safely.

It was 0200 when the three hit the sleepy town of Portland. The three shadowy figures who emerged from the car didn't hesitate. They were like children having decided to jump into a freezing mountain spring. They headed for the house, their faces firmly set toward the door.

Alton rang the doorbell and knocked until a light appeared within. A gruff voice challenged them through the door. "What in the world do you want? Do you realize what time it is?"

Blake was undeterred. "Is your name Lloyd Simpson?"

"Yes, what of it?"

"We have a friend who needs your blood," Sonny spoke plainly.

"Mr. Simpson," Blake tried to explain. "We have a friend who served with us in World War II. He saved our lives. Now he's lying in the hospital near death because they don't have the blood to match his rare type. His blood's the same as yours, Mr. Simpson," Blake continued, his voice choked with emotion. "You're the only one who can help him. If you don't come with us, Sam Shepherd won't live through the night."

Suddenly the door flew open and Lloyd Simpson emerged. "Would that be the same Sam Shepherd who piloted the *Wind Walker*?" he asked.

Three surprised friends shouted in unison, "Yes!"

Lloyd disappeared again, leaving the men standing dumbfounded on the steps. In a minute he reappeared wearing a robe, moving at full speed, and bellowing, "What are we waiting for? Let's get going. We have a hero to save."

On the way to the hospital, Lloyd showed them a picture of himself with Sam standing in front of the *Wind Walker*'s hangar. Lloyd had been a mechanic at the air base. He had never forgotten Sam because once, when he had been seriously wounded, Sam had come to his rescue. It was Sam's blood that had sustained Lloyd's life. He could scarcely believe that now, after all these years, he would have the chance to return the favor.

Chapter Three: *commitment*

It was nearly four o'clock in the morning when the Roadmaster reached the hospital with its precious cargo. Sam was fading fast when the doctors rushed Lloyd in for the transfusion.

Several more hours passed before the doctor appeared with a cautious smile on her weary face, bearing the news that Sam's bleeding had finally stopped. But he wasn't out of the woods yet.

Now it was early in the morning—just a few hours after their middle-of-the-night mission to save Sam's life—when they gathered to wait for news at their favorite coffee shop. They had just raised their cups when Alton's cell phone rang. Answering it with a timid hello, his face soon broke into a big smile. "He's all right then?" Alton laughed in relief.

He hung up the phone, then dialed the number for Lloyd, who had since been released from the hospital. "Lloyd?" he said after a moment of silence. "I wanted you to get the news when we all did. Sam is going to be fine." They all erupted in cheers.

When they settled down, Alton continued: "Sam's wife told him what you did for him, Lloyd. He wants us to stop by during visiting hours. He wants you to come too. He also told me to ask you one more thing: What are you doing on Tuesday mornings?"

Chapter Four

Involvement

a sense of concern with
and curiosity about
someone or something

*Y*ou don't have to *fear* evil.
I *restore* your soul and
prepare blessings for you
in the *presence* of your enemies.

*B*ecause I help you,
you won't be disgraced.
I am your sun and your shield,
giving you *grace* and *glory*.

*I*n the shelter of My presence,
I hide you
from the intrigues of people
and *protect* you
from false accusations.

God of Truth

DEFINING YOU,

Your God of Truth

PS Remember, I am for you! Who can be against you?

—from Psalm 23:3–5; Isaiah 50:7;
Psalms 84:11; 31:20; Romans 8:31

$\mathcal{D}$o you know what your friends say about you? You may be surprised. They may not talk much about your looks or your charm. They probably don't even focus on your taste in clothes or the car you drive. No, when your friends talk about you, they speak about different qualities. Perhaps they describe you as having eyes that are always watchful; you never miss a thing when it comes to friends who are in need. Your eyes are constantly on the lookout for ways to serve and protect those for whom you care.

Or maybe they comment on your hands—how busy they are, always waving to neighbors, greeting new people and inviting them into your world. Your hands never seem still; they are actively engaged in offering needed affection or comfort.

They might even describe your feet as being swift, running toward tragedy or heartbreak, getting you there first and without fail. And when you arrive, your bright and sympathetic smile warms the heart and welcomes the hurting.

What may surprise you the most is how many of your friends notice your voice: calming when the storms of doubt arise; encouraging when others are weary; inspiring when someone's courage begins to falter; hopeful when goals and dreams seem hard to attain.

Oh, sure, you're nice looking, smart, maybe even witty—but your friends recognize that your most valuable quality is your willingness to get involved in the lives of others. To make a difference. To be a friend.

A true friend provides
a safe haven. She accepts us,
failures, foibles, and all.
She does not judge us when
we show her who we are.
She responds with
gentleness and empathy.
She is genuinely on our team.

Ann Hibbard

*E*lizabeth ran down the steps and into the street, arriving just as the young driver pulled a baseball bat from his backseat and started for the older man.

Friendly Intervention

*T*o look at Elizabeth, you'd think she was sugar sweet and calm spirited. Everyone who knew her well would agree…to a point. Elizabeth Kilcher, with black hair reaching down to her shoulder blades, large brown eyes, delicate frame, and quick step, was genuinely kind and easygoing. But on a warm July evening, two strangers were about to find out what Elizabeth's friends and family already knew.

It was just about dusk in the small suburb of St. Louis, Missouri. Elizabeth was washing the dinner dishes and gazing out her kitchen window overlooking the street in front of her house. She loved to look at the beautiful yard sculpted and nurtured by her husband, Stan. That evening, he had gone to an important meeting with the leadership of their church. Elizabeth stayed behind with their two sons, who were watching their favorite program on television in the living room.

Suddenly Elizabeth heard the ugly sound of metal crunching and folding, like the sound of one of her boys flattening an empty soda can. She caught a glimpse of two cars at the intersection just down the street. As she leaned in closer to the window, she saw two men step out of their cars. One looked to be in his late forties, dressed in khaki slacks and a denim shirt. He towered over the other, younger man who glared back at him. The boy couldn't have been more than eighteen years old. He wore baggy blue jeans, a black-and-white T-shirt with "No Fear" printed on it, and a scowl that spelled trouble.

Elizabeth could tell that the two were yelling at each other about the fact that the older man had rear-ended the young man's car. It was clearly the older man's fault, since the teenager was stopped at the intersection waiting for his turn to proceed. Their argument was escalating to fever pitch, and if allowed to continue, it looked as though it would end in violence.

Elizabeth dashed into the living room and instructed the boys to stay put; she had to go outside and would be right back. But her agitated tone made the boys lose all interest in the program and follow her outside to see what was going on. From their front porch, the family heard a fountain of profanity from the older man. He was denying responsibility for the accident and blaming the young man for not pulling out sooner.

The young driver's verbal counterattack had a harshness and intensity that made Elizabeth's hair stand on end. The older man said something derogatory about the boy's mother. The young man's face flushed a terrible shade of red, and he turned back and walked swiftly toward his car.

In a flash Elizabeth sensed what he was doing. Until then, she'd been unsure whether she should get involved in this scene. Now she knew she had to step in. She ran down the steps, across the small front yard, and into the street, arriving at the scene just as the young driver pulled a base-ball bat from his backseat and started for the older man. Elizabeth stepped in between them, placed both hands against the boy's chest, and leaned hard to keep him from advancing farther. "Son, I don't know you, but I'm telling you right now that you don't want to ruin your life by assaulting the likes of this guy."

The teenager, with angry tears forming in his eyes and pronounced veins throbbing in his neck, spoke through clenched teeth. "He said something about my mother that I can't let him say."

"I know," Elizabeth said, trying to calm him. "I heard him myself. But his behavior doesn't give you the right to physi-cally attack him. Look at him," she said, nodding red-faced toward the other driver. "He's old enough to know better, and yet he talks and acts like some irresponsible child."

"Hey, lady, what business is this of yours?" the man piped up, insulted.

friendly intervention

Elizabeth swung around to face the man, pointed up to her porch and said, "You see those boys up there? Well, I'm their mother, and I will not have you invading their world with anger and language they shouldn't have to hear."

The man scowled with anger at his injured pride and aimed a challenge at the boy: "Come on with that bat, if you want to!" The boy surged forward, but Elizabeth was once more able to block him and hold him off.

"Listen," she spoke more firmly this time. "Your mother, whom you're defending, would tell you to back off—not to attack this idiot, because he's not worth it. You don't want to throw away your future on him, do you?" she pleaded, now holding his gaze and speaking more gently.

The young man looked into Elizabeth's sincere brown eyes and saw his own mother's care reflected in them. Realizing she was right, he turned sullenly and headed back to his car.

Elizabeth turned once more toward the older man and scolded him: "You ought to be ashamed of yourself, assaulting this boy with such profanity. She waved her hand around, indicating the neighbors who had gathered. Everyone can see that the accident was your fault.

"Grace, call the police," she shouted to her elderly friend across the street. Elizabeth wasn't about to leave until the situation was completely diffused. She then left the man by his car and walked back to talk with the teenager once more.

By now the young driver's anger had subsided, and other emotions took its place. "Thank you, ma'am," he repeated over and over as tears streamed down his face. "If you hadn't been here, I know I would have killed him. I just know I would have killed him."

Elizabeth learned that the young man's name was Kevin, that his mother had recently died after a long illness, and that Kevin had been struggling to adjust after the loss. She tried to comfort him. "Kevin, your mom would have been proud of the choice you made today."

After the police ticketed the older man and both drivers left the scene, Elizabeth walked back to her home to the applause of everyone who had witnessed her courage. This was the Elizabeth they had come to know—someone who would intervene in any situation where someone was in need—especially in need of a friend and advocate.

Elizabeth didn't consider her work done, however. She started shopping at the grocery store where Kevin worked so she could check on him and offer support and encouragement. Kevin always made sure he was the one to carry out Elizabeth's groceries so he could have a chance to update her on what was going on in his life. The two became good friends, always sharing a short prayer together before they parted. Many times Kevin would close her car door and lean down to the window, not wanting anyone else to see his misty eyes, and say, "Thanks again, Mrs. Kilcher, for being there when I needed you the most."

"Friends look out for each other," she would always answer, smiling warmly. "That's just what we do."

Chapter Five

Sacrifice

forfeiture of something highly valued
for the sake of one considered
to have a greater value or claim

*B*ecause of My incomparable
love for you,
I made the **ultimate** sacrifice,
giving up My *Son*.

*Y*ou can **trust**
Me to *graciously* give
you **all things.**

*L*ove each other
as *I've loved* you.
Love others **sincerely** and *deeply,*
honoring others above yourself.
Real love is **patient** and kind
and isn't *self-seeking.*

*T*he hidden **blessing** is that
when you *delight* yourself in **Me,**
I give you the **very** things
your **heart** truly *desires.*

GIVING MYSELF FOR YOU,

Your

King and

Friend

—from Romans 8:32; 1 John 4:7; 1 Peter 1:22;
Romans 12:10; 1 Corinthians 13:4–5; Psalm 37:4

*S*elf-sacrifice is the defining pinnacle of friend-ship. Jesus said, *"Greater love has no one than this, that he lay down his life for his friends"* (John 15:13).

We're not often called upon to sacrifice our lives for our friends, but the principle of sacrifice remains true today. If you have friends you know would brave a burn-ing car to pull you to safety or face down an angry mob that was after your blood, you can count yourself blessed indeed. But sacrifice is so much more than being willing to die for a friend.

It's being willing to die *with* your friend when the crowd condemns or ridicules your ideas. It's accommodating your craving for Chinese when she's secretly dying for pizza. It's driving across town three times a day to let your dog

74

out so you can have a romantic weekend away.
It's giving you the best seat at the movies, the bigger piece of French silk pie, and taking vacation to accompany you to the doctor for that scary test.

Sometimes we might not even be aware of the loving sacrifices a friend is making on our behalf. That's what was so awesome about Jesus' sacrifice: He gave His life to save those who didn't know Him or who rejected Him as their friend.

Sacrifice for a friend is always worth it, even if it's never acknowledged, appreciated, or known. No sacrifice is ever unnoticed. Be assured that Jesus, our example, sees the sacrifices you make for your friends and will reward you in the end.

If you really love one another, you will not be able to avoid making sacrifices.

Mother Teresa

Concern for her friend's pain
trumped Lauren's own.
She felt powerless to change anything.

Best-Dressed Friends

*L*auren looked out at the bright spring day, opened the window of her van, and let the fresh warm air rush over her. She had looked forward to this day for nearly two months. At times she had found herself smiling in anticipation of unveiling the secret she had planned for her best friend. She glanced back at the mysteriously cloaked item hanging from the hook over the backseat. Rosemary and her husband, Randall, were renewing their vows today. It was a delicious opportunity to repay the kindness Rosemary had shown

Lauren nearly twenty years before. As she drove, Lauren's mind went back to the day of their junior prom—an event that had sealed their loyalty and expressed their love for each other.

Two local high school boys had captured their hearts and asked them to the prom. Rosemary's date was Randall Beasley, her steady for almost a year and a half. For them, this prom held special significance because the following month, Randall was going to the West Coast to join the marines. It was their last high school event together; then he would be gone for two years.

Lauren's date was Tyler Cross. They had met while working on a school play three weeks earlier. Lauren was sure it was true love. Tyler was graduating but staying in the area to attend college. This would be their first big event together, and Lauren was looking forward to every moment.

The girls shopped together to find their dream dresses for the prom. Rosemary chose a hot pink, fitted dress—strapless and covered with sequins. Lauren chose a yellow chiffon, Cinderella-style gown with a sweet satin choker.

They convinced the boys that they should go as a foursome, and for the next two weeks, they spared nothing as they planned to make this the most meaningful night of their lives.

The morning of the prom, Lauren and Rosemary had their hair done at an upscale beauty shop downtown, then spent the afternoon giving each other manicures. They giggled and chatted incessantly about the evening.

They indulged in hours of primping: putting on makeup, perfume, lotions, and hair ornaments. The climax of the afternoon was the moment when they slipped into their dresses and stood before the full-length mirror. They were stunning. They admired themselves and agreed that glamour suited them well.

When the boys arrived and Rosemary's mother went to open the door, the girls ran to the top of the stairs and began their descent with an air of practiced sophistication. They had rehearsed their entry several times throughout the day because they felt clumsy in their heels and wanted to get it just right.

Chapter Five: *sacrifice*

Suddenly Lauren's heel caught in the hem of her dress. She grabbed the rail in a desperate attempt to keep from falling. But a nail sticking out from one of the vertical posts snagged her dress. It ripped a jagged tear from her knee all the way to her hem as she stumbled down two steps before catching herself. The girls gasped. The yellow chiffon was beyond repair. She couldn't possibly go to the prom with her dress in this condition.

Recognizing Lauren's grief, Tyler tried his best to comfort her. He suggested they both change clothes and go somewhere nice to eat. But his words were met by muffled sobs. Tears filled Lauren's eyes. She felt her whole evening falling apart. The four sat down on the stairs. They were silent, except for Lauren's quiet sobbing.

"You know, Tyler is right," Rosemary finally said with more cheeriness than anyone felt. "It's just a silly old prom. We don't need it to have a good time or make good memories. Let's all change and go out to dinner."

"No," Lauren protested. "You're going to the prom, and that's all there is to it. I know what this means to you with

Randall going away next month. It's the end of an era. You can't stay home on my account."

Rosemary smiled at her and said, "OK, we'll go. I'd want you to go if something happened to me. Will you at least walk me to the car?"

"Sure," Lauren said, sniffling and wiping tears from her cheeks with the back of her hand.

Rosemary took one step down the stairs, and her heel gave way. "My ankle!" she screamed. "I think I broke it!"

Lauren grabbed her arm, incredulous that this could really be happening. "What can I do? Tell me what to do," she insisted.

"Help me up," Rosemary whimpered. "I don't know if I can walk."

When she tried to stand, her ankle gave out completely, and Rosemary collapsed back onto the step. "I can't walk. I can barely get up." Rosemary began to cry softly. "Lauren, could you and Tyler please get me an ice pack from the freezer? Randall, would you carry me to my bedroom?"

Concern for her friend's pain trumped Lauren's own. She

felt powerless to change anything and so was grateful for even this small assignment to help.

As Lauren and Tyler retrieved the ice pack, she couldn't help trying to figure out what he was thinking. She didn't imagine he'd ever ask her out again after all the troubles he'd seen tonight. Lauren pushed the sadness from her mind and focused on Rosemary.

They hurried back and ran into Randall at the top of the stairs. "I think it's just a sprain," he told Lauren, "but she's in a lot of pain. She could use that ice pack right now."

Lauren rushed to Rosemary's side. "Listen," Rosemary told her. "I want you to wear my dress and go to the prom. There's no reason for both of us to miss it."

"No," Lauren objected. "I'll stay with you."

"Randall and I decided that we'd rather be alone tonight, since he's leaving so soon. It's settled, Lauren. You and Tyler are just starting out. Randall and I are old hands at this. We have last year's prom to remember." Rosemary's tone was firm. "I won't take no for an answer."

When the switch had been made, Rosemary teased affectionately as she admired Lauren in her dress. "If you were a real friend, you'd never consent to looking better in my dress than I did!"

The girls giggled, but Lauren grew somber. "I don't like this."

Rosemary squeezed her hand. "You go have fun for both of us tonight. I mean that. If you come back telling me you were miserable, you'll ruin it for both of us. Now get out of here. I want every detail when you get home."

Lauren did precisely what Rosemary asked and had the time of her life at the prom. Just before midnight, Lauren had Tyler drop her off at Rosemary's house unannounced. Through the picture window, Lauren saw Rosemary and Randall dancing. Rosemary's limp had mysteriously disappeared, and judging by her graceful movement, she was in no pain.

Lauren's face flushed hot with a sudden realization. She was tempted to barge in and scold her friend for tricking her.

But that would ruin the evening for everyone, she decided. Rosemary's was an act of devotion, and she would keep the secret until she found the perfect way to pay her back.

That day finally arrived—twenty years later.

Lauren pulled up to Rosemary's house. Chairs for the big event were set up under a large white tent in the yard. Rosemary turned to greet her. She was wearing a plain cotton dress with summer sandals and a wide-brimmed hat. Lauren knew Rosemary had wanted to buy a special gown for the ceremony, but times had been tough recently, and she wouldn't even hint of it to Randall.

Rosemary was radiant with joy. "Where's the family?" she asked.

"Oh, they'll be here soon, but I wanted to come early. I have a secret to share with you." Lauren reached inside her van and pulled out her surprise. She removed the plastic cover to reveal a beautiful, white satin wedding dress—the one she had worn to marry Tyler fifteen years ago. Rosemary gasped, speechless.

best-dressed friends

Lauren draped the dress across Rosemary's arms. "Nearly twenty years ago," she explained, "you faked an injury to trick me into wearing your dress to the prom. You gave me memories to last a lifetime. Now I'm giving you my most special dress—along with some plane tickets for a weekend in Chicago—to help you celebrate a lifetime of memories."

Rosemary buried her face in Lauren's shoulder and wept tears of joy. Lauren scolded her affectionately for smudging her makeup with sentimentality. As Rosemary retreated eagerly to put on the gown, Lauren reminded her: "If you're a real friend, you'll never consent to looking better in my dress than I did!" Rosemary turned to hug her. Lauren squeezed her friend tightly. "Now get out of here," she told her. "I'll want every detail when you get home."

Chapter Six

Dependability

the trait of being
dependable or reliable

I've planned and *know*
all of your days.
My eyes *search* the earth
to strengthen you when your *heart*
is fully *devoted* to Me.

*E*ven if your body or your
emotions break down,
you'll have **peace** knowing that
I am the strength
of your **heart** and
your *destiny* forever!

*Y*ou, in turn, demonstrate
My greatest *love*
when you **sacrifice** your life
for your *friends*.

KEEPING MY COVENANT
OF LOVE WITH YOU,

Your

Ever Present

God

—from Psalms 139:16; 73:26; John 15:13; Deuteronomy 7:9

*W*henever your friends mention you, it's in connection with these five words: I can always depend on… And with good reason.

Truer words could not be spoken. You're the first to arrive and the last to leave, the first to give and the last to take. When crisis comes to a friend's life, it's your name that immediately comes to mind as someone on whom a person in need can call. You always seem to know what to do, even in the worst of circumstances. When faced with hard questions, your friends know that either you'll have the answer or you'll search until you find it. If a battle is raging, you will bring peace. If someone's heart aches, you will bring healing.

You live like the one who said, *"Come to me, all you who are weary and burdened, and I will give you rest"* (Matthew 11:28). But Jesus didn't always wait for those in need to come to Him. Sometimes, He went to them. When His friend Thomas was confused and doubting, Jesus went to him. When the women who were His friends were grieving, He went to them. Jesus' friends learned that they could depend on Him.

Like Jesus, when others won't—or can't—come to you, you go to them. Many lives have been blessed by your help in times of need. And those who call themselves your friends know: They can always depend on you.

$\mathcal{F}$riends are God's hands

extended to help.

They find joy, freely going

the extra mile to

help a friend in need…

just because they care.

LeAnn Weiss

*B*eth tried to scream, but the man
clamped his hand over her mouth
to muffle the sound.

The Winning Team

Lori and Beth's friendship had come easily. It had its beginning on a snowy November day in Colorado Springs when they were both just entering junior high. Beth was tall, athletic, and sweet-natured. Lori was petite and a bit sassy, with little interest in athletics. They had few things in common aside from their shoulder-length, sandy blond hair and expressive smiles—and a healthy sense of determination.

The girls had been paired together in gym class for a two-on-two basketball competition. Their opponents were the class snob, Heidi Hostettler, and her best friend, Susan Blake—both excellent players. Heidi was Lori's social nemesis, and Lori hated losing to her and her partner. Heidi and Susan were hardly graceful winners, and they could be obnoxious during the games.

Beth had only recently relocated and joined the school, and no one had seen her play; but all assumed from her soft appearance that she would be the weakest link in this match. "Easy win here, Susan," Heidi said to her teammate loud enough for Lori and Beth to hear.

Beth immediately sensed the tension between the girls, leaned over to Lori, and said, "Hey, you want to beat these girls?"

"Yeah, more than anything, but they're too good," Lori lamented.

"Well, I'm not a bad ball player. You get me the ball inside. We can beat this team—together." Beth's assured manner was inspiring and contagious, and the girls set out to win.

Within minutes it was clear that Lori was teamed with

one of the best basketball players in the school, and during the time they played, Beth even made Lori look like a star. The two former snobs hung their heads as they walked away with beaten egos at the short end of a 20 to 6 score. Lori and Beth had clinched both a victory and a friendship.

Throughout high school and college the girls were insepa-rable, their close friendship almost making them seem like one person instead of two. They called each other's parents Mom and Dad, and the two were rarely seen apart. They double-dated on most occasions and fell in love with another pair of best friends, Donny and Pat. But the most characteristic sign of their friendship was that somehow, as though they could read each other's minds, Lori and Beth always were there for each other.

It was during their senior of year of college that Beth was walking across campus to meet Lori and cut through an area called Christy Woods. She had taken that path a hundred times, but never this late at night. About halfway through the woods, she sensed danger, but she tried to calm herself by rationalizing that she was probably imagining things. Suddenly a figure leaped from behind some trees and attacked her. She tried to scream, but the man clamped his hand over her mouth to muffle the sound. All kinds of frightening thoughts raced through her mind as she tried to fight off her assailant.

Then, without warning and right beside her, Beth heard a familiar voice: "Hey, creep, chew on this for a while!" With a swift, solid crack, a heavy limb was swung with great force against the dark figure. Lori had come up behind the attacker and landed a blow so hard it sent him sprawling and then running away.

In hysterical relief, Beth lunged at Lori and hugged her so tightly she nearly shut off circulation in Lori's arms. "How did you know, Lori? How did you know I was out here in trouble?" Beth asked between sobs.

"I'm not sure, Beth—I just had a feeling, and I'm glad I followed my hunch! I love you, girl, and I don't want anything bad to happen to you."

Beth couldn't help but break into tearful laughter. "You really scared him off!"

"Hey, we can beat anything—together," Lori smiled. The two friends hugged again, then Lori escorted Beth to the police station to report the incident.

After college, Beth married Donny and moved to Seattle, Washington, where they had three boys and Donny built a career with Boeing. Lori married Pat, moved to Nashville, and had two girls and a boy while Pat built his career in the country-music industry. Though Beth and Lori stayed in touch at first, time and distance eventually had their way, and the two friends fell out of communication.

Several years later, Lori was driving home on a hot summer day when a truck crossed the centerline of the highway and forced her car off the road and into a tree at sixty miles per hour. Her legs were crushed, and she suffered a collapsed lung and several other serious internal injuries. She was rushed to the hospital, but within twenty-four hours, her kidneys started shutting down.

Chapter Six: *dependability*

A doctor explained that Lori would need a kidney transplant and then delivered the grim news that the waiting list was nearly two years long. The hospital staff would try to keep her system functioning through dialysis until a matching donor organ could be found.

But Lori's condition worsened overnight, and she awoke the next morning to a roomful of bustling nurses that seemed to be preparing her for something. But through her confusion and growing panic, Lori heard a familiar voice. "Hey, you want to beat this thing?" Beth came into her line of vision, wearing the same indomitable smile she had worn when she took on the challenge of that first basketball game.

"Yeah, more than anything," Lori responded with tears and the mixed emotions of joy in the reunion and fear of the future. "But I think it's bigger than both of us."

"Well, I've got a pretty good kidney here that the doctor says will fit you perfectly," Beth answered in her familiar, assured manner. "And once you get that, I think we stand a chance." She squeezed her friend's hand with affection.

Lori was amazed at her friend's willingness to share a kidney—and at her timing. "But how did you know I was in trouble? Did Pat call you?"

"No, I just woke up yesterday and sensed that you needed me, so I called. Pat filled me in on what had happened. I caught the next flight to Nashville, and I'm glad I did! I love you, girl, and I don't want anything bad to happen to you." Beth was teary-eyed now too and hugged her friend gently. "We beat the class snobs, we beat the attacker in the woods, and we'll beat this too—together."

Chapter Seven

Faithfulness

the quality of adhering firmly and
devotedly, as to a person, cause,
or idea; loyalty

*K*now that I **never** stop *guarding* you and *tenderly* **watching** over *you.*

I command My **angels** concerning your *protection.* I'll **never** leave or *give up* on you.

*E*ven when **you** are faithless, you can *count* on My **steadfast** commitment.

My love for you **endures** forever, and My *faithfulness* **continues** through all *generations.*

FOREVER FAITHFUL,

Your
God of
Refuge

—from Psalms 121:8; 91:11; Joshua 1:5; 2 Timothy 2:13; Psalm 100:5

*F*aithfulness is a hallmark of friendship. It takes many forms, but perhaps the most treasured faithfulness in friendship is silence. Not a lack of communication but a communication without words. In friendship, there are times when words don't need to be spoken because friends know each other. They hear heart cries as audibly as vocal ones. And, even when a need is unspoken, they faithfully respond.

Many things can mute our cries for help, support, or encouragement. Shame, regret, and fear are silencers. Yet true friends respond faithfully, enabled by special sensors that are alerted at the smallest telltale sign of need. If someone is missing without reason, a friend starts searching. If someone is sad or weighed down by circumstances, a

friend will faithfully come alongside to help
lift the load. If someone fails, a friend faithfully
forgives—whether or not a confession is offered.

Pain—even unexpressed pain—is felt and shared by
faithful friends. They understand unspoken fears and
offer assurance. Friends can sense the storms of suffering
that ravage your heart, and they offer shelter. True
friends faithfully fulfill the needs that go undetectable
by most. Friends rush to your side without a syllable
being uttered.

Friends talk about their thoughts, feelings,
dreams, fears, and needs. They share laughter
and tears. But the best friends are the ones
who, through years of faithfulness, know
us well enough to understand and
respond even when we're quiet.

A faithful friend

is a strong defense;

and he that hath found him

hath found a treasure.

Louisa May Alcott

*J*esse wouldn't have moved on to
another location without notifying them—
something had to be terribly wrong.

The Friendship Adventure

The three friends met at Woodstock in 1969. Seth, lean and tan with shoulder-length blond hair, had come for the music. Rebecca, tall and fine-featured with brunette hair and a model's sense of fashion, had come for the excitement of being at a historical event. Jesse, a southern wit who wore a baseball cap to cover his receding hairline, hitchhiked from Indiana to satisfy his hunger for adventure.

Bone weary, hungry, and thirsty, this unlikely trio met on the second night of the concert at a campsite far enough from the music to allow for conversation. After sharing the small amounts of food they had brought, they began to share their dreams, disappointments, and discoveries in life. When they learned that they lived only a short distance from each other in Indiana, the small group decided to share a bus ride home and to stay in close contact after that. As darkness fell over the camp, the light of friendship dawned in their hearts, and they became devoted soul mates.

Shortly after Woodstock, the three friends began meeting each weekend at Seth's apartment just north of Indianapolis. From there they would launch out on two-day adventures they took turns planning. When it was Seth's turn to schedule the events, the weekend was always filled with music. Often the trio attended concerts, cooked out to the sounds of their favorite artists, or went to out-of-the-way coffeehouses to hear the songs of some unknown artist.

Rebecca's weekends were wild, fast paced, and event driven: the Indianapolis 500, Fan Fair in Nashville, state fairs all over the country. Rebecca seemed to have a sense for where excitement could be found or where history was being made, and she knew how to get there.

When it was Jesse's turn at the wheel of leadership, he never ceased to amaze the other two with adventures into what he called God's sculptures on earth. The group would hike into wooded country, climbing to the top of secluded summits. Jesse's favorite weekends consisted of camping trips into the Smoky Mountains, where the three marveled at the surrounding nature and wildlife.

One particular trip into the Smokies stood out as one of their most exciting. They had started with a hike to the Chimneys, a high summit upon which stood three natural towers that offered a magnificent view of the vast mountain range. Then the three friends moved deeper into the forest to enjoy some of the most magnificent and secluded waterfalls in the park. They even ventured into some innocent but dangerous play with some bear cubs while their mother watched cautiously from a distance. This interaction with nature left them misty-eyed when it came time to return to "normal" life.

Chapter Seven: *faithfulness*

Seth, Rebecca, and Jesse developed a bond that made them more like siblings than mere friends. They were there for each other in the good times and the bad. When Rebecca's widowed mother passed away, Seth and Jesse came to help with the funeral arrangements and to stand with Rebecca as friends and neighbors filed by to pay their respects.

When Seth lost his job and was unemployed for a couple of months, Jesse and Rebecca picked up his rent and helped pay for food and utilities. After landing a good job, when Seth tried to repay them, Rebecca and Jesse refused. "Oh, we'll get the money back someday when we're in trouble, believe us. We won't forget," they insisted. But Seth knew they would.

Jesse was the only one who seemed to escape real trouble. That is, until the spring of 1973. On a rare weekend when the threesome couldn't divest themselves of other commitments, Jesse decided to take a solo trip to the Smokies. He was going through some soul searching and felt sure he would find answers in the seclusion of the mountains. He called Seth and Rebecca to let them know he was going, then set off on his excursion on Friday night.

On Sunday night, when Jesse should have returned home and normally would check in with his friends, Seth and Rebecca thought it was odd not to hear from him. They sensed that something was wrong, so they both arranged to take time off from work and headed for Tennessee. When they arrived they immediately notified the authorities. The two friends had to work to convince the rangers that Jesse wouldn't have just moved on to another location or extended his trip without notifying them—that something had to be terribly wrong.

After a series of phone calls confirming with Jesse's family that he had not been in contact with them either, search-and-rescue teams were organized and sent out. The forest service launched a massive effort, but no one could find Jesse. Days went by. Seth and Rebecca were exhausted from covering the rough terrain, and by Thursday evening authorities decided to call off the three-hundred-member search party. The nights had been unusually frigid, even for that high elevation, and experts felt certain it was too late. All hope that Jesse was alive somewhere in those mountains was gone...except for the hope in Seth and Rebecca's hearts.

The two friends were determined not to leave Jesse behind, alone in the woods—no matter what. They went into an outfitter in Knoxville and bought all the equipment they would need for an independent search. At first light on Friday morning, the pair stood at the base of the mountains and paused for a moment of prayer for their friend and for their rescue efforts. Then they set off toward the Chimneys. That was Jesse's favorite spot, and though they had covered that area before, they felt sure that would be the place they'd find Jesse.

Seth and Rebecca searched until dark, shouting Jesse's name every few feet until they were hoarse, hoping against hope that they would hear some response. Nothing. They spent that night around a campfire, alternately dozing and praying silently, and always listening for Jesse's voice.

Saturday was more of the same. More walking, more calling out, more silence. That night the two friends momentarily considered giving up. But they knew Jesse would never give up if it were them, and they determined that they wouldn't give up either.

Late Sunday evening, just when Seth and Rebecca were about to head back into town for fresh supplies, they heard a faint voice. Immediately they knew it was Jesse. Weariness replaced by adrenaline, they moved swiftly in the direction of the distant cry and kept calling out to Jesse, telling him to keep calling their names—they were coming. Within a few minutes, they came upon a wounded, bleeding, and nearly lifeless Jesse. They could see immediately that he had been mauled by a bear. He had somehow managed to drag himself to a shallow cave to take cover and await rescue.

Seth and Rebecca dropped to their knees and wrapped their arms around Jesse in grateful reunion and relieved sobs, thanking God that they had, at last, found their friend alive. Then they worked quickly to bandage Jesse's wounds and get liquid and nourishment into his dehydrated body.

Finally safe in the hands of his trusted friends, Jesse allowed tears to flow freely. He was so weak from his ordeal that he could barely speak, but Jesse motioned for Seth and Rebecca to come close. With a strained whisper Jesse spoke to his friends, pronouncing each word slowly and deliberately: "I knew you'd never give up until you found me. Thank you, friends. I love you both."